This Book Belongs To

_____

In Loving Memory Of

_____

A GRIEF JOURNAL IS A BEREAVEMENT DIARY WITH DAILY WRITING PROMPTS AND SPACE FOR REMEMBRANCE TO HELP YOU MOVE THROUGH LIFE AFTER THE LOSS OF YOUR DEAR LOVED ONE.

LOSING SOMEONE YOU LOVE DEARLY CAN BE A DIFFICULT SITUATION TO DEAL WITH MENTALLY AND EMOTIONALLY.

THIS GUIDED PROMPTS WORKBOOK JOURNAL HOPES TO PROVIDE A WAY TO EXPRESS THOSE THOUGHTS ON PAPER AND CREATE A MEMORY BOOK TO CHERISH THE MEMORIES.

Your Daily prompt

Favourite times together

Daily thoughts.

Stick your favourite time together here

Thoughts from the heart

Clear you mind and relax while colouring

Your Daily prompt

Favourite meals

Daily thoughts.

Make your loved ones favourite meal.
Take a picture and Stick it here.

Write down all your thoughts by mindmapping here:

Write a poem showing your emotion. ♡

_____

_____

_____

_____

_____

_____

_____

_____

_____

_____

Your Daily prompt

Daily thoughts.

Favourite jokes

Write your favourite joke said by your loved one here.

Thoughts from the heart

Clear you mind and relax while colouring

Write down all your thoughts by mindmapping here:

Make a list of things you want to get done this week.

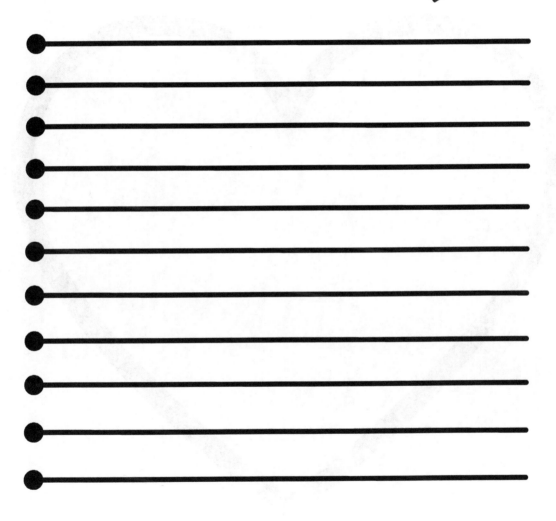

Thoughts from the heart

Your Daily prompt

Name of all your children here

Daily thoughts.

- ✖
- ✖
- ✖
- ✖
- ✖

Stick Your Family Picture here

Use this space to draw what ever is on your mind.

Write down all your thoughts by mindmapping here:

Clear you mind and relax while colouring

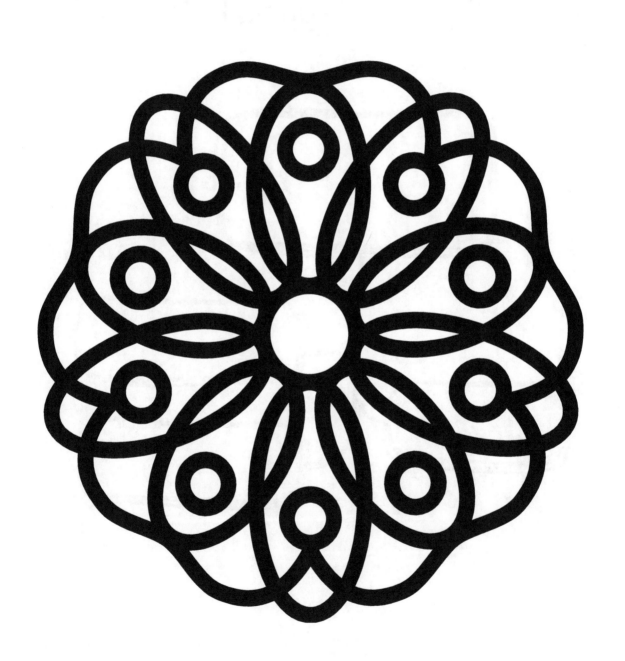

List all the things you loved about your Lost Loved one.

♡

-
-
-
-
-
-
-
-
-
-
-

Thoughts from the heart

Write down all your thoughts by mindmapping here:

Your Daily prompt

Favourite Holidays Together

Stick your Favourite Holiday Picture Here

Clear you mind and relax while colouring

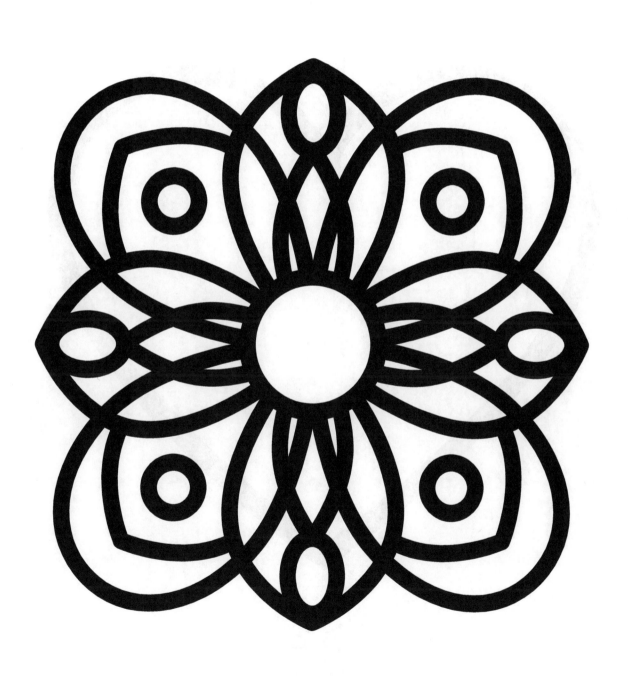

Thoughts from the heart

List all the things your Loved one used to annoy you with.

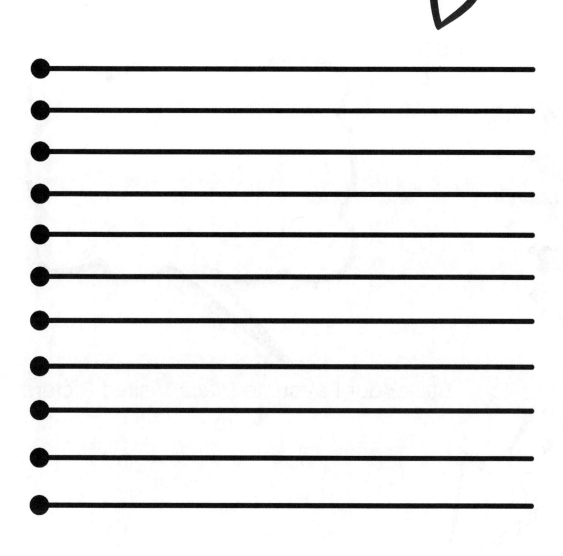

Thoughts from the heart

Write a letter for your
lost love
one
expressing
all your thoughts and emotions!.

Get your letter
typed and laminated and place your thoughts
next to your loved ones
grave, so they know how you feel
at all times.

All is well

Death is nothing at all,
I have only slipped into the next room
I am I and you are you
Whatever we were to each other, that we are still.
Call me by my old familiar name,
Speak to me in the easy way which you always used
Put no difference in your tone,
Wear no forced air of solemnity or sorrow
Laugh as we always laughed at the little jokes we enjoyed together.
Play, smile, think of me, pray for me.
Let my name be ever the household word that it always was,
Let it be spoken without effect, without the trace of shadow on it.
Life means all that it ever meant.
It is the same as it ever was, there is unbroken continuity.
Why should I be out of mind because I am out of sight?
I am waiting for you, for an interval, somewhere very near,
Just around the corner.
All is well.

www.ingramcontent.com/pod-product-compliance
Lightning Source LLC
LaVergne TN
LVHW071558160125
801479LV00011B/748